AMANDA

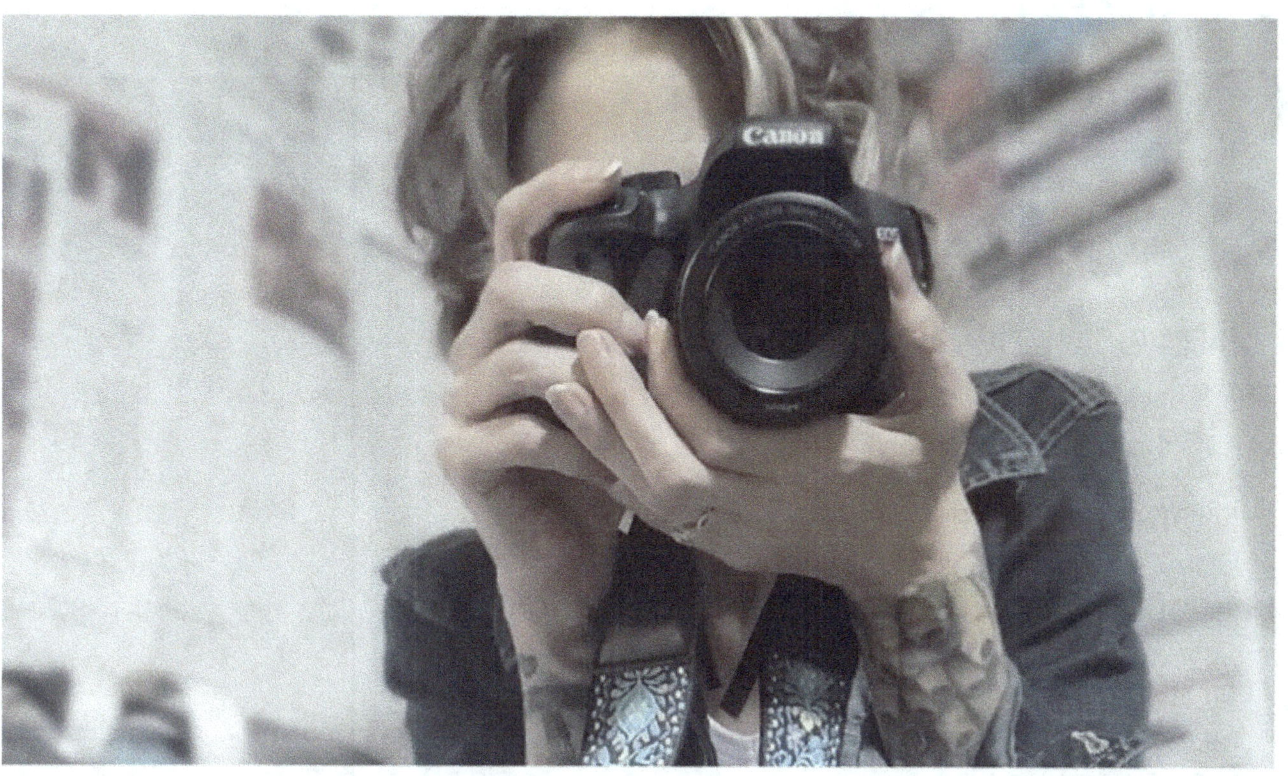

Amanda Otis, photographer

Hi, my name is Amanda and am a photographer. I have always had a love of photography and a few years ago, finally purchased my first professional camera.

I've spent the last few years taking pictures of just about everything, learning alot and growing my portfolio. I would describe my style as bold, true color along with contrast.

I am a published freelance writer and photographer, providing portrait, product, and real estate photography services.

I also coach others on creating digital products to generate additional, passive income for their businesses.

And I can help you too!

Reach out via email if you have any questions about creating digital products or my digital product creation coaching packages.

Email:
be.photography,indiana@gmail.com

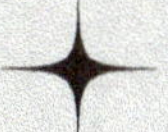

TABLE OF CONTENTS

IN THIS E-BOOK, WE'LL COVER HOW TO BUILD AN ONLINE BRAND. WE'LL GO OVER THE BASICS OF BUILDING A BRAND, AND THEN DIVE INTO SPECIFICS FOR CREATING YOUR OWN.

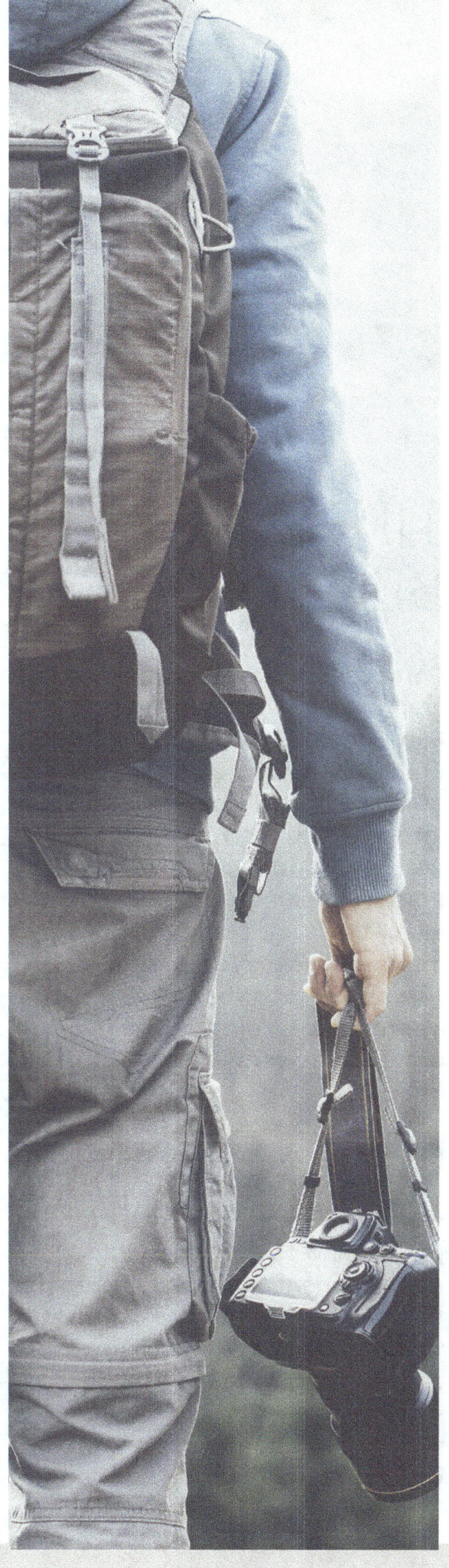

01

INTRODUCTION

In a world where visuals speak volumes, your photography portfolio becomes your voice and your ticket to success in the world of photography. Whether you're an aspiring photographer looking to break into the industry or a seasoned pro aiming to refresh your body of work, creating a compelling photography portfolio is an art form in itself.

So, grab your camera, unleash your creativity, and let's dive into the world of portfolio building, where every click of the shutter brings you one step closer to crafting a portfolio that truly stands out in the crowd.

LET'S DO THIS!

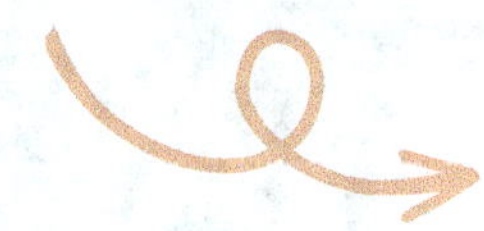

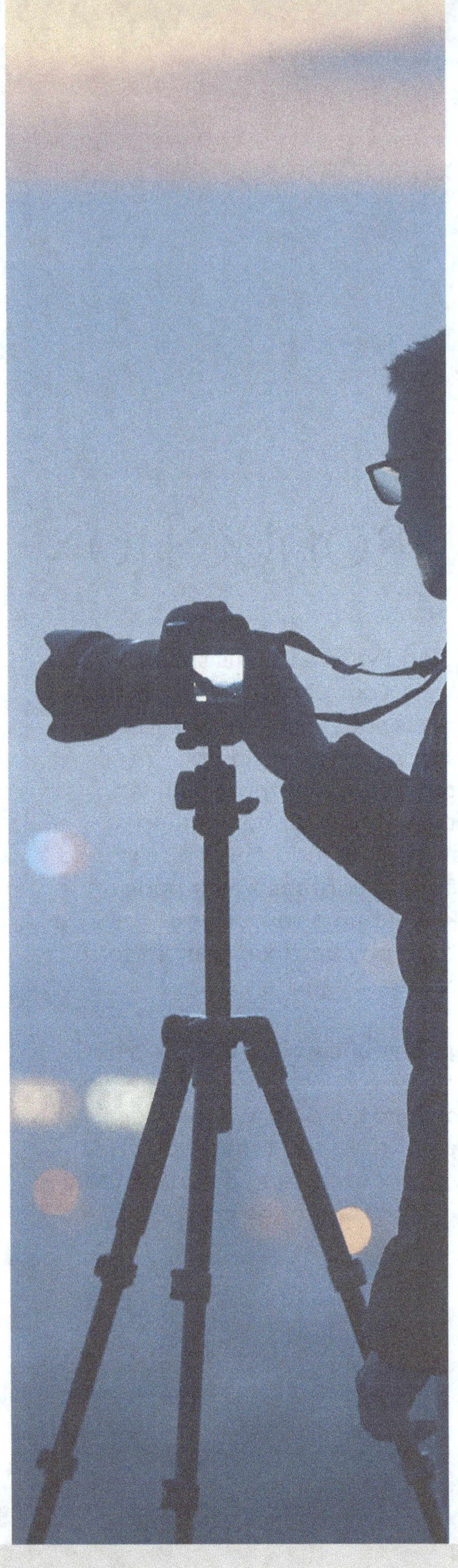

02

TIPS FOR BEGINNERS

Composition plays a crucial role in creating captivating images. Familiarize yourself with the rule of thirds, a simple but effective guideline that divides your frame into nine equal parts using two horizontal and two vertical lines. Place your subject or key elements along these lines or at their intersections to create visually pleasing compositions. Pay attention to leading lines, which draw the viewer's eye into the image.

Experiment with different angles and perspectives to add depth and interest to your shots. Lastly, be patient and observant; wait for the right moment, and don't be afraid to take multiple shots to capture that perfect image. Photography is as much about creativity and storytelling as it is about technical skill, so practice and explore to develop your unique style.

LEARN MANUAL MODE

Shooting in manual mode can seem daunting at first with all of the different settings and such, but I recommend learning manual mode from the start.

Get acquainted with the exposure triangle and start shooting in manual mode right from the start. Manual mode gives the photographer complete control over the light, aperture, and speed the photograph is taken, helping you to create the exact image you are seeing in your head.

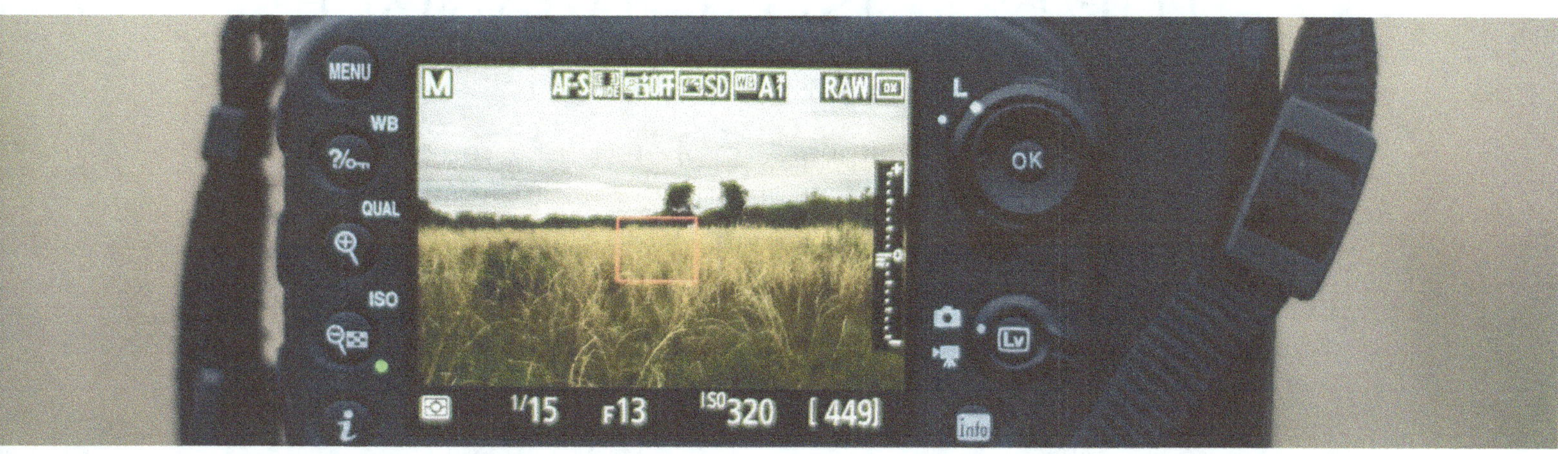

ADVANTAGES OF MANUAL MODE

Manual mode is especially valuable in challenging lighting situations. For instance, when shooting in low light, you can use a wide aperture (low f-number) to allow more light in and a slower shutter speed to capture more light over a longer duration, all while keeping ISO as low as possible to minimize noise. In situations where you want to control both the depth of field and motion, like photographing a subject against a blurred background while freezing their movement, manual mode lets you find the perfect balance.

While it may seem intimidating at first, shooting in manual mode empowers you to achieve creative and technically precise results, making it a valuable skill for any photographer to acquire. With practice and experimentation, you'll unlock the full potential of your camera and elevate your photography to the next level.

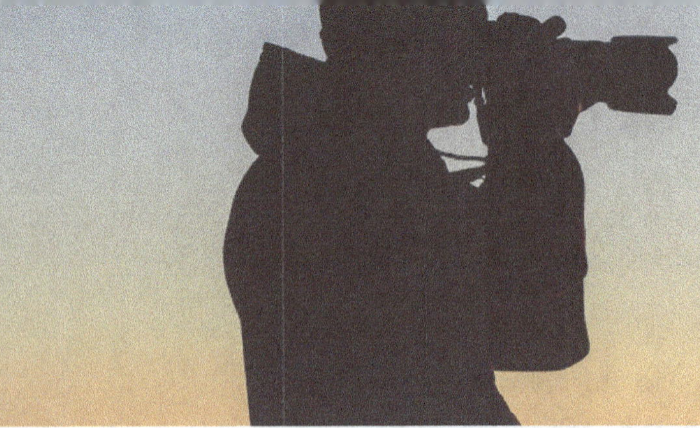

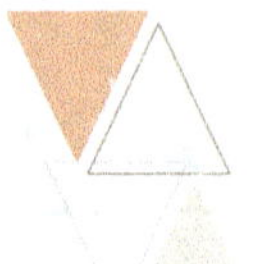

THE EXPOSURE TRIANGLE

To fully understand the fundamentals of photography, you must learn about the three main components of exposure: aperture, shutter speed, and ISO.

Aperture controls the amount of light entering the camera, affecting depth of field; a lower f-number (e.g., f/2.8) results in a blurred background, while a higher f-number (e.g., f/16) keeps more in focus.

Shutter speed determines how long the camera's sensor is exposed to light; faster shutter speeds freeze motion, while slower ones create motion blur.

ISO relates to your camera's sensitivity to light; lower ISO settings (e.g., ISO 100) are ideal for bright conditions, while higher ISOs (e.g., ISO 800 or above) help in low light but can introduce noise. Experiment with these settings to understand their impact on your photos.

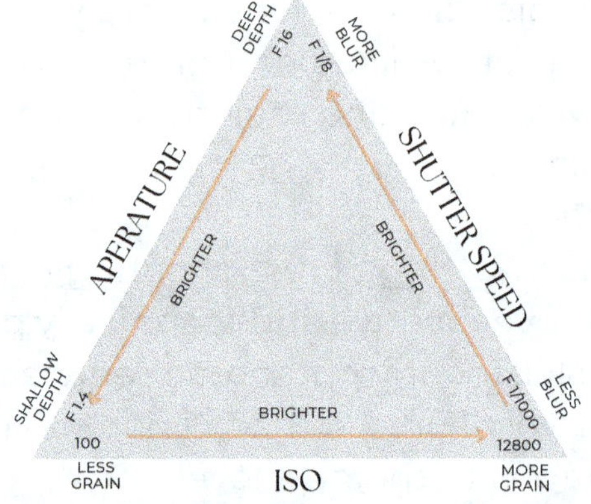

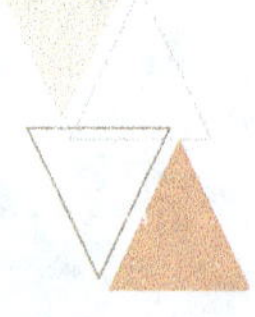

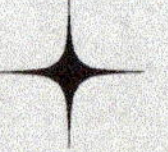

MORE SHOOTING TIPS

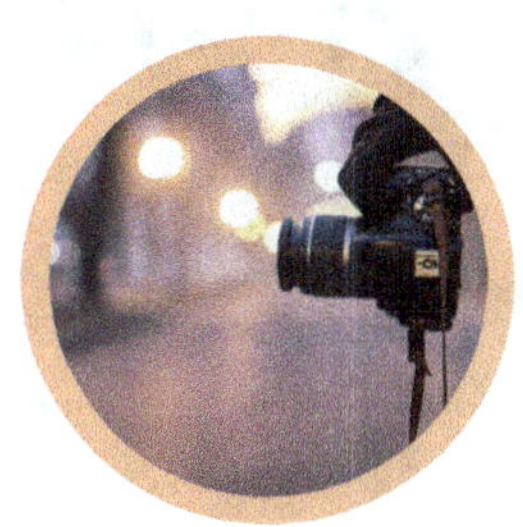

TAKE YOUR CAMERA EVERYWHERE & SHOOT DAILY!

I am sure you've heard it before...because it's true! Practice makes progress so take your camera everywhere with you and shoot daily. Look for scenes, spaces, people, and things to capture in your daily life to hone your skills and familiarize yourself with your camera so that shooting becomes like second nature.

EXPLORE DIFFERENT GENRES OF PHOTOGRAPHY

Experiment with various photography genres such as landscape, portrait, wildlife, street, real estate, product photography, and more to diversify your portfolio and help decide what type of photography you love the most! Different genres of photography call for different lenses, settings, and editing techniques to make your photos the best they can be. Practicing each of these genres will build different photography skills, making you a better photographer and editor.

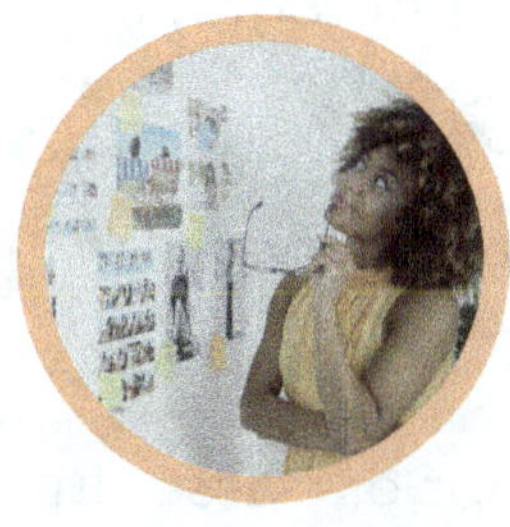

CREATE PERSONAL PROJECTS FOR SHARING

Create personal photography projects or styled shoots to add insight into your photography journey. This can be a great way to not only connect with potential clients, showing them where your passions and interests lie, but also allowing your creativity to flow without limits. No client wishes or demands, just pure artistic creation!

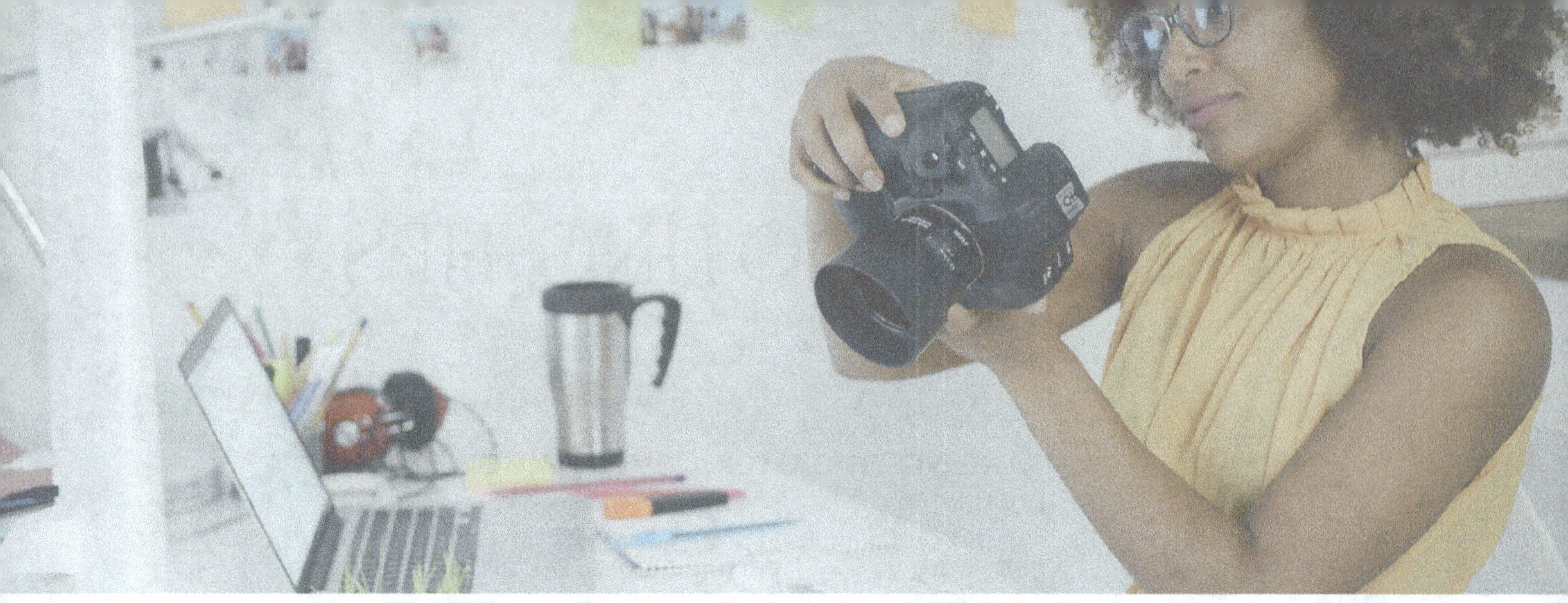

LEARNING RESOURCES

Photography learning resources are essential for both beginners and experienced photographers looking to enhance their skills and knowledge. These resources come in various forms and cater to different learning preferences. Here are some valuable photography learning resources:

1. **Online Tutorials and Courses**: The internet is a treasure trove of photography tutorials and courses. Websites like Photography Life [3], Storius Mag [6], and Click Photo School [2] offer a wide range of free and paid tutorials on photography basics, advanced techniques, and specialized genres. You can learn at your own pace and choose courses that align with your interests and skill level.

2. **Photography Books**: Photography books authored by renowned photographers provide in-depth insights into the art and craft of photography. Books like "Understanding Exposure" by Bryan Peterson and "The Photographer's Eye" by Michael Freeman offer valuable tips and techniques for photographers of all levels. You can find these books at your local library, bookstore, or as e-books.

3. **Photography Workshops**: Attending photography workshops or classes in your community can be a hands-on and interactive way to learn. Many photography enthusiasts and professionals offer workshops that cover various topics, from camera settings to composition and post-processing. Check with local photography clubs or institutions for workshop opportunities.

LEARNING RESOURCES (CONT.)

4. **YouTube and Online Communities**: YouTube hosts countless photography channels that provide tutorials, gear reviews, and photography tips. You can also join online photography communities and forums like Reddit's r/photography [5], where photographers share their experiences, ask questions, and offer advice.

5. **Photography Apps**: Mobile photography has become increasingly popular, and there are apps like Adobe Lightroom and VSCO that offer powerful tools for editing and enhancing your photos. These apps often come with built-in tutorials to help you get the most out of your smartphone photography.

6. **Photography Magazines**: Photography magazines like "National Geographic" and "Digital Photography Review" feature stunning images and articles that can inspire and educate. Subscribing to such magazines can keep you updated on the latest photography trends and techniques.

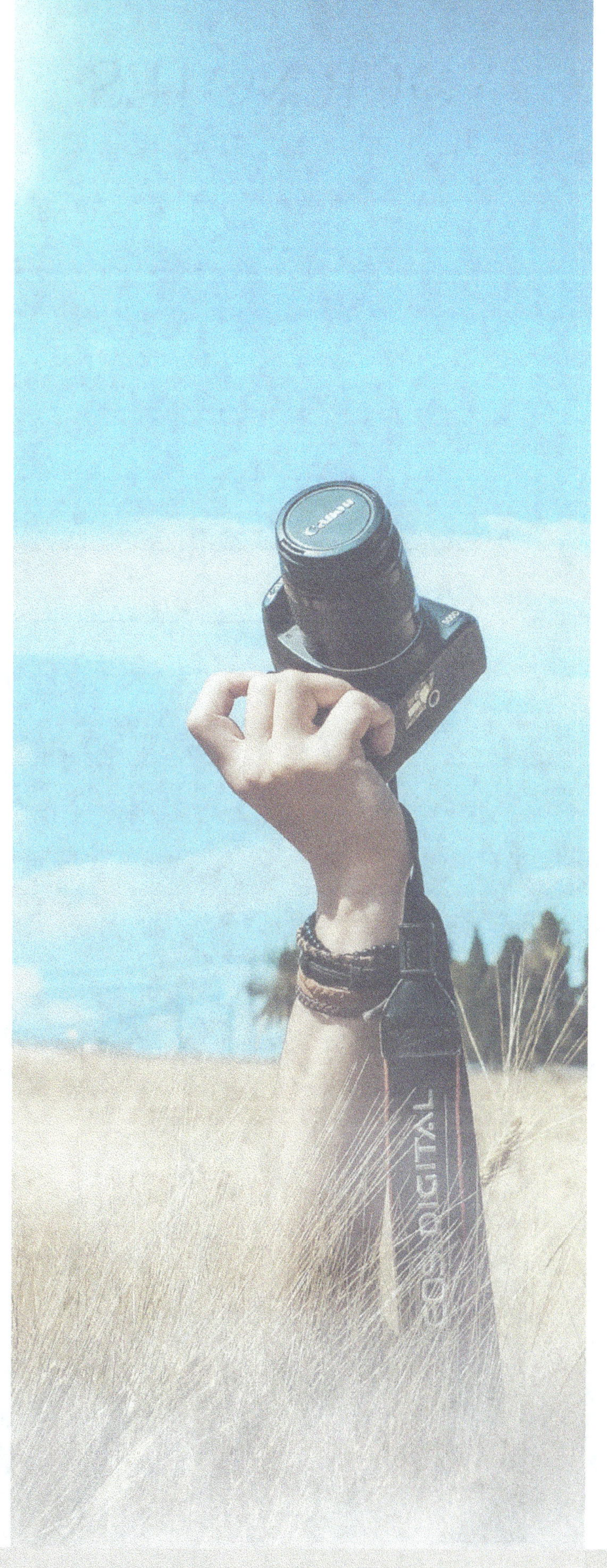

YOUR NOTES:

____

____

____

____

____

____

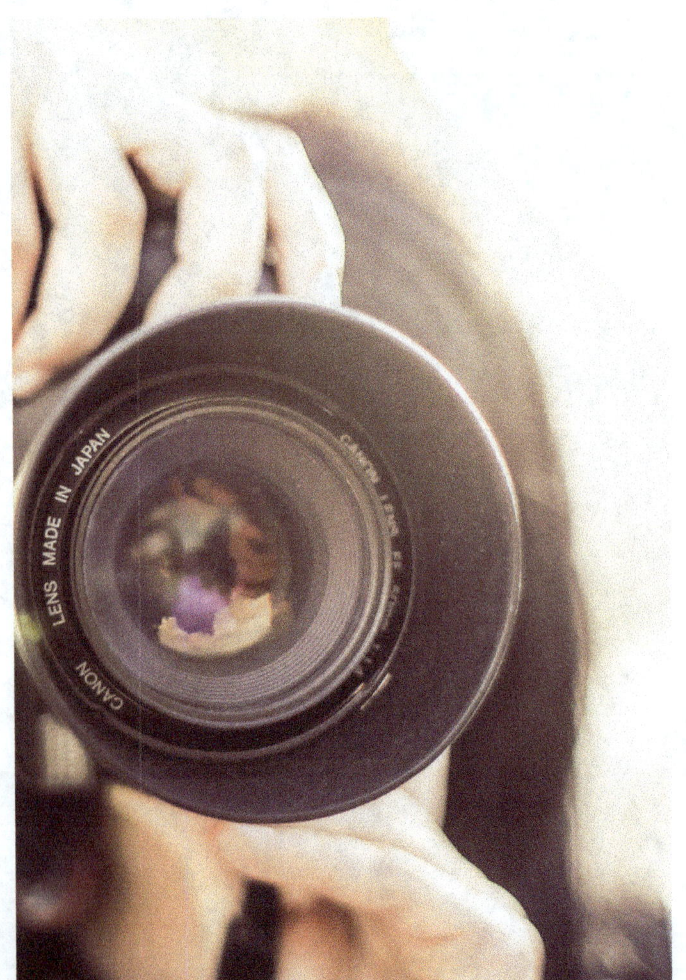

LASTLY, HAVE FUN!

Remember that photography is both an art and a craft, and it's perfectly okay to make mistakes and learn from them. Embrace the joy of discovery, and your love for photography will only deepen as you continue to grow and develop your skills.

Enjoy the process!

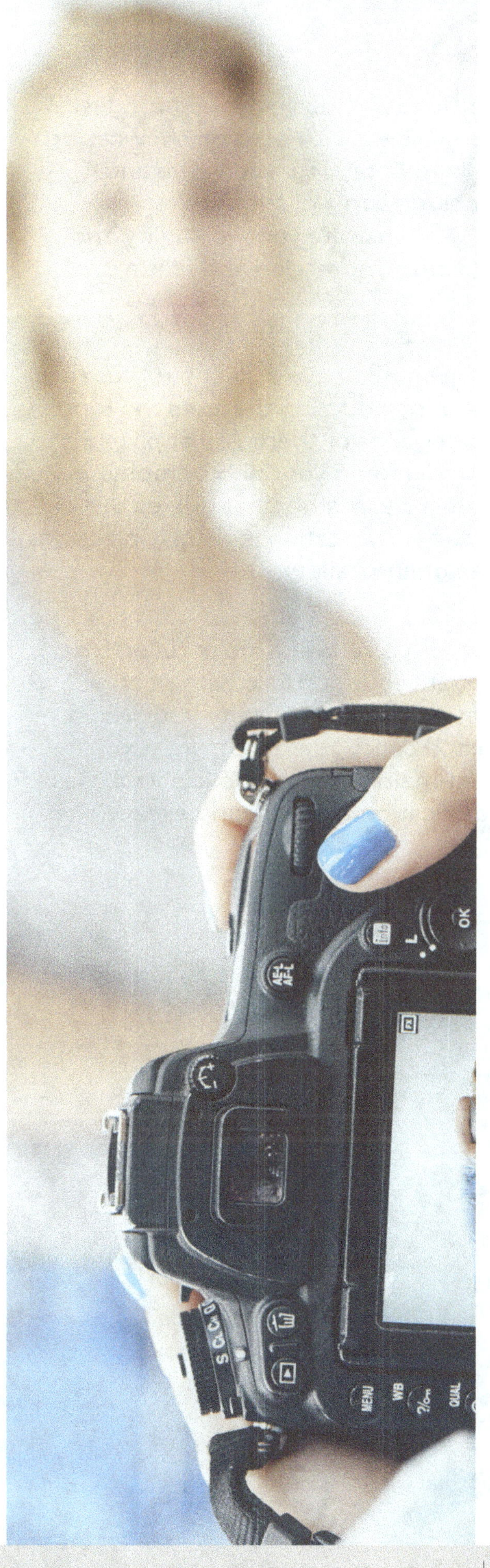

03

BUILDING A PHOTOGRAPHY PORTFOLIO

A photography portfolio is a carefully curated collection of your best images that represent your body of work and showcase your unique style and abilities as a photographer. It serves as a visual resume and a means to communicate your vision, talent, and expertise to potential clients, employers, or anyone interested in your photography. A well-organized portfolio not only highlights your technical proficiency but also conveys the story you want to tell through your images.

The first step in building a photography portfolio is choosing your strongest
images. Quality always trumps quantity, so be selective. Focus on showcasing
a diverse range of your skills and styles while maintaining a cohesive and
consistent look throughout the portfolio. Include a mix of subjects,
compositions, and lighting conditions that demonstrate your versatility and
creativity. Aim for a portfolio that leaves a lasting impression and tells a
compelling visual narrative.

The organization of your portfolio is crucial. It should have a clear structure and
flow. Begin with a captivating cover image or introduction that sets the tone
for your portfolio. Arrange your work into categories or themes, if applicable, to
make it easier for viewers to navigate and understand your photography.
Consider the sequencing of images to create a visual story that guides the
viewer through your portfolio. Ensure that the presentation is visually pleasing,
whether in a physical printed portfolio or an online gallery.

A photography portfolio is not static; it should evolve over time to reflect your
growth and changing style. Periodically update your portfolio with new,
stronger work, and remove any images that no longer align with your vision.
Seek feedback from peers, mentors, or trusted colleagues to ensure your
portfolio remains fresh and engaging. A well-maintained portfolio showcases
your commitment to your craft and your dedication to producing exceptional
photography.

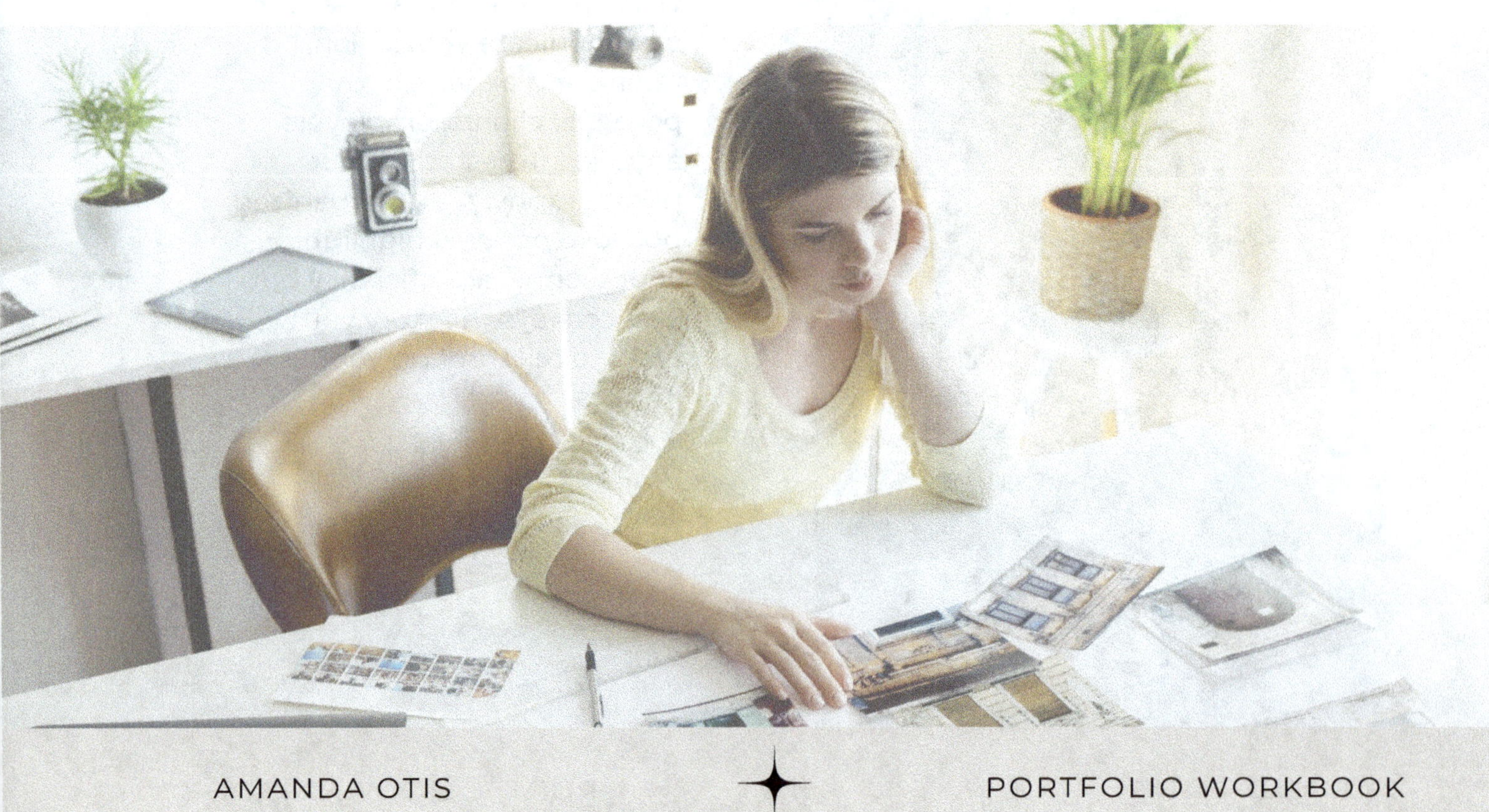

PORTFOLIO-BUILDING ACTIVITIES

THE PORTFOLIO-BUILDING ACTIVITIES IN THIS SECTION OF THE WORKBOOK WITH HELP YOU PRACTICE & IMPROVE:

1. COMPOSITION & FRAMING
2. LIGHTING & EXPOSURE
3. SUBJECT & GENRE CHALLENGES
4. TECHNICAL SKILLS
5. STORYTELLING & CONCEPTUAL
6. PHOTOGRAPHY
7. POST-PROCESSING & EDITING
8. PERSONAL GROWTH & CREATIVE CHALLENGES

THESE EXERCISES WILL NOT ONLY HELP YOU BUILD YOUR PHOTOGRAPHY SKILLS BUT ALSO DIVERSIFY YOUR PORTFOLIO WITH A RANGE OF CAPTIVATING IMAGES.

REMEMBER THAT PRACTICE, EXPLORATION, AND CREATIVITY ARE KEY TO BECOMING A MORE SKILLED AND VERSATILE PHOTOGRAPHER.

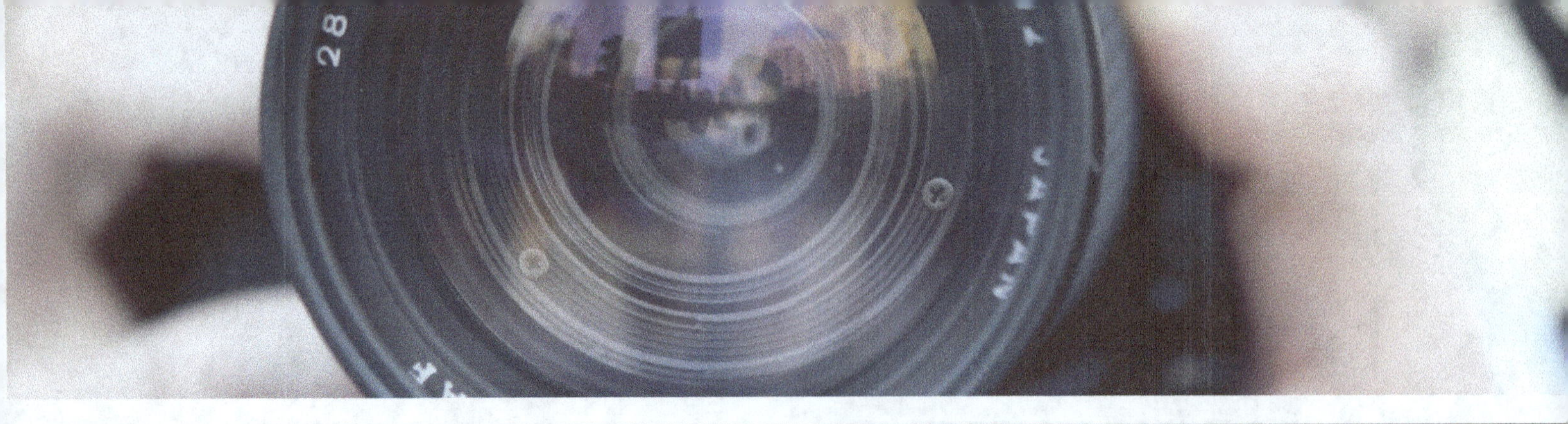

50 PHOTOGRAPHY PORTFOLIO-BUILDING EXERCISES

Here are 50 photography exercises and challenges to help you enhance your skills and build an impressive portfolio:

COMPOSITION & FRAMING

1. **Rule of Thirds:** Compose images using the rule of thirds for balanced and visually appealing shots.
2. **Leading Lines:** Find and photograph natural or architectural lines that lead the viewer's eye.
3. **Symmetry:** Capture symmetrical scenes, showcasing balance and order.
4. **Golden Hour:** Shoot during sunrise or sunset to harness the soft, warm light.
5. **Frame Within a Frame:** Look for natural frames (e.g., doors, windows) to emphasize your subject.
6. **Minimalism:** Create powerful images with minimal elements.
7. **Fill the Frame:** Get close to your subject to emphasize details.
8. **Negative Space:** Use negative space to highlight your subject.
9. **High and Low Angles:** Experiment with shooting from high and low perspectives.
10. **Diagonal Lines:** Incorporate diagonal lines for dynamic compositions.

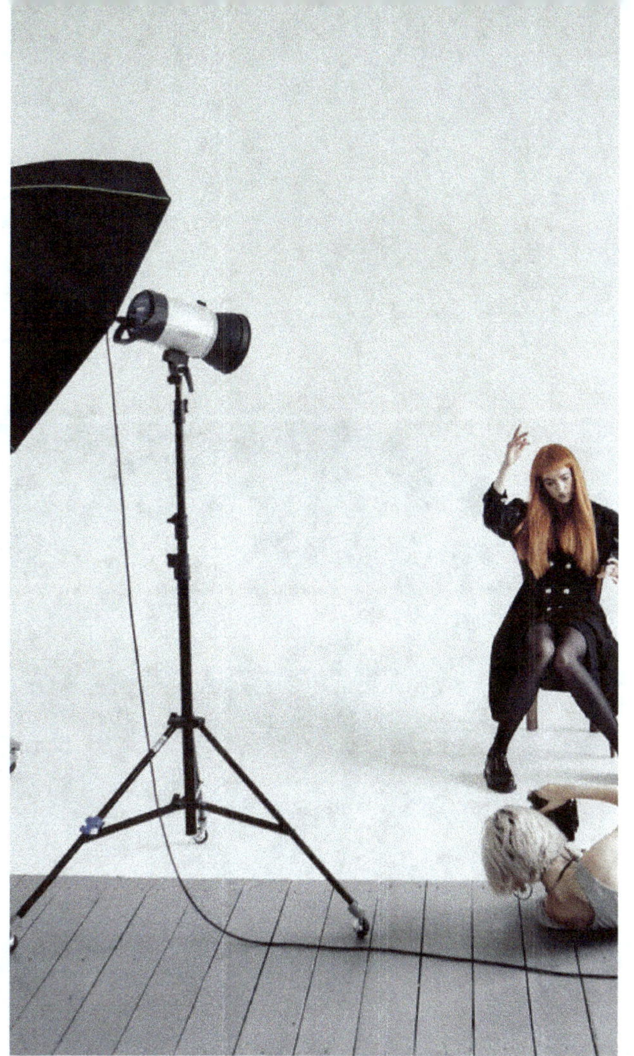

LIGHTING & EXPOSURE

11. **Silhouettes:** Capture striking silhouettes against a bright background.
12. **Low Light Photography:** Practice shooting in low-light conditions without flash.
13. **Backlighting:** Experiment with shooting against the light source for creative effects.
14. **High Key and Low Key:** Explore high key (bright and airy) and low key (dark and moody) photography.
15. **Natural Light Portraits:** Master outdoor portrait photography using natural light.
16. **Light Painting:** Create captivating images by painting with light in long-exposure shots.

YOUR NOTES:

SUBJECT & GENRE CHALLENGES

7. **Street Portraits:** Approach strangers and take candid street portraits.
18. **Reflections:** Find and capture interesting reflections in water, glass, or shiny surfaces.
19. **Texture Photography:** Highlight textures by photographing close-ups of different surfaces.
20. **Motion Blur:** Convey movement by using slow shutter speed for dynamic shots.
21. **Color Splash:** Isolate a single color in a black-and-white image for emphasis.
22. **Double Exposure:** Experiment with in-camera or post-processing double exposures.
23. **Still Life:** Create compelling still life arrangements and experiment with lighting.
24. **Urban Exploration:** Explore and document abandoned or interesting urban spaces.
25. **Nature Macro:** Capture intricate details of insects, plants, or other small subjects.
26. **Night Sky Photography:** Learn astrophotography techniques to capture the stars and Milky Way.

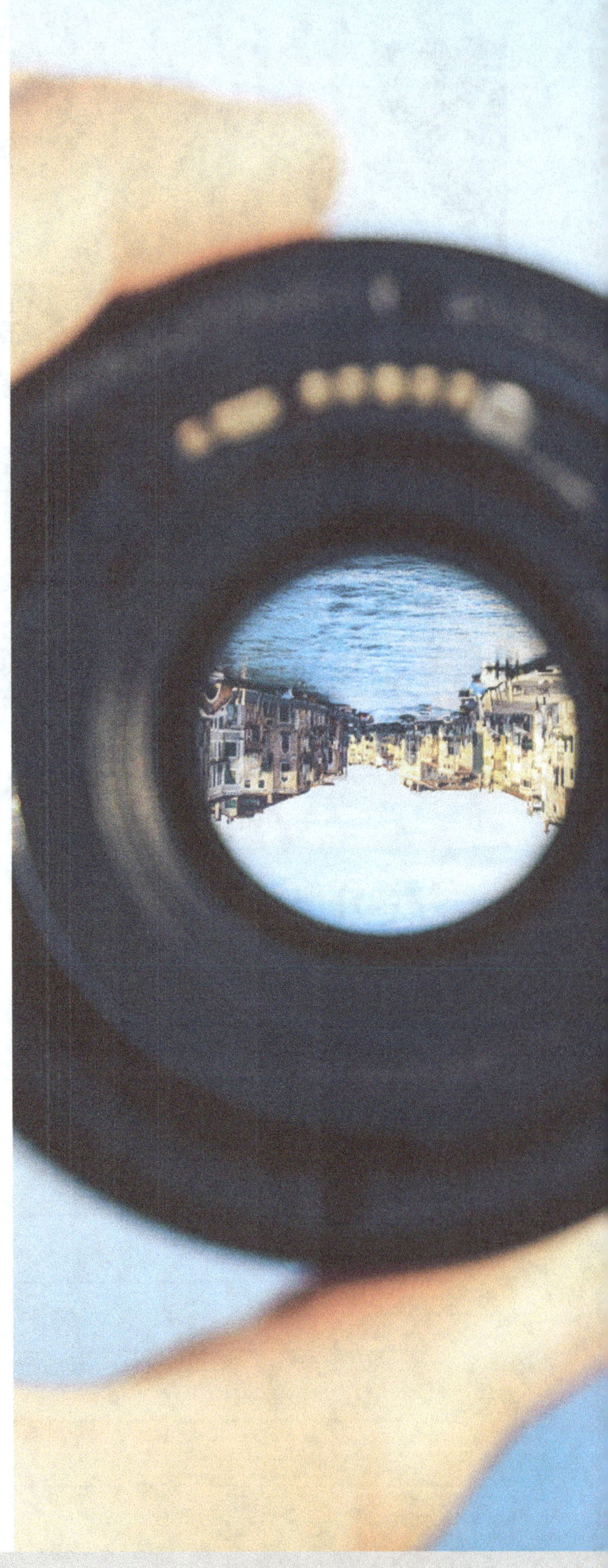

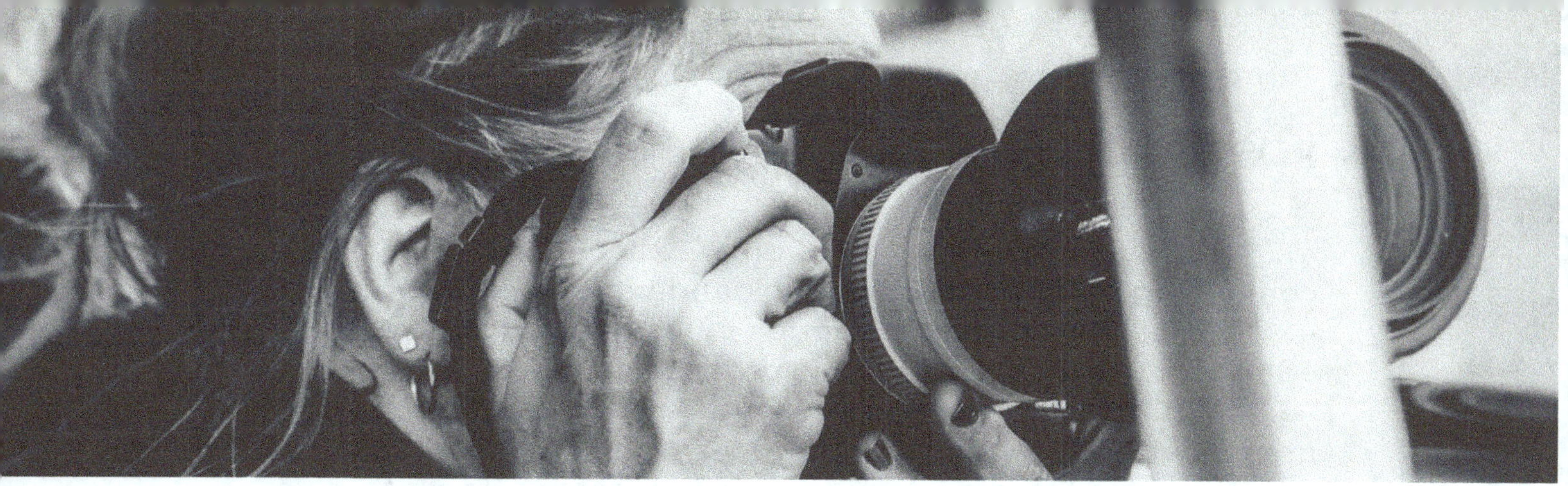

TECHNICAL SKILLS

27. **HDR Photography:** Try High Dynamic Range (HDR) techniques for scenes with extreme lighting.
28. **Panorama Stitching:** Create panoramic images by stitching multiple shots together.
29. **Bokeh:** Achieve beautiful bokeh (background blur) using wide apertures.
30. **Long Exposure Waterfalls:** Capture silky-smooth waterfall shots with long exposures.
31. **Freeze Motion:** Use fast shutter speeds to freeze fast-moving subjects.
32. **Bracketing:** Practice exposure bracketing for varied results.
33. **Focus Stacking:** Combine multiple shots with different focus points for sharp images.
34. **Forced Perspective:** Experiment with this technique to create optical illusions.

STORYTELLING & CONCEPTUAL PHOTOGRAPHY

35. **Photo Series:** Develop a series of images that tell a cohesive story or convey a concept.
36. **Emotions:** Portray a range of emotions in a series of portraits.
37. **Juxtaposition:** Combine contrasting elements to convey a thought-provoking message.
38. **Day in the Life:** Document a day in your life or someone else's through photographs.
39. **Narrative Self-Portrait:** Create a self-portrait that tells a personal story.
40. **Time-Lapse Story:** Tell a story through a time-lapse sequence.

POST-PROCESSING & EDITING

41. **Black and White Conversion:** Experiment with converting color images to black and white.
42. **Color Correction:** Practice color correction and enhancing techniques in post-processing.
43. **HDR Processing:** Learn to merge and tone-map HDR images effectively.
44. **Vintage Effect:** Apply vintage or retro effects to give photos a timeless feel.
45. **Selective Color:** Isolate specific colors while converting the rest to black and white.
46. **Composite Images:** Create composite images by combining elements from multiple photos.

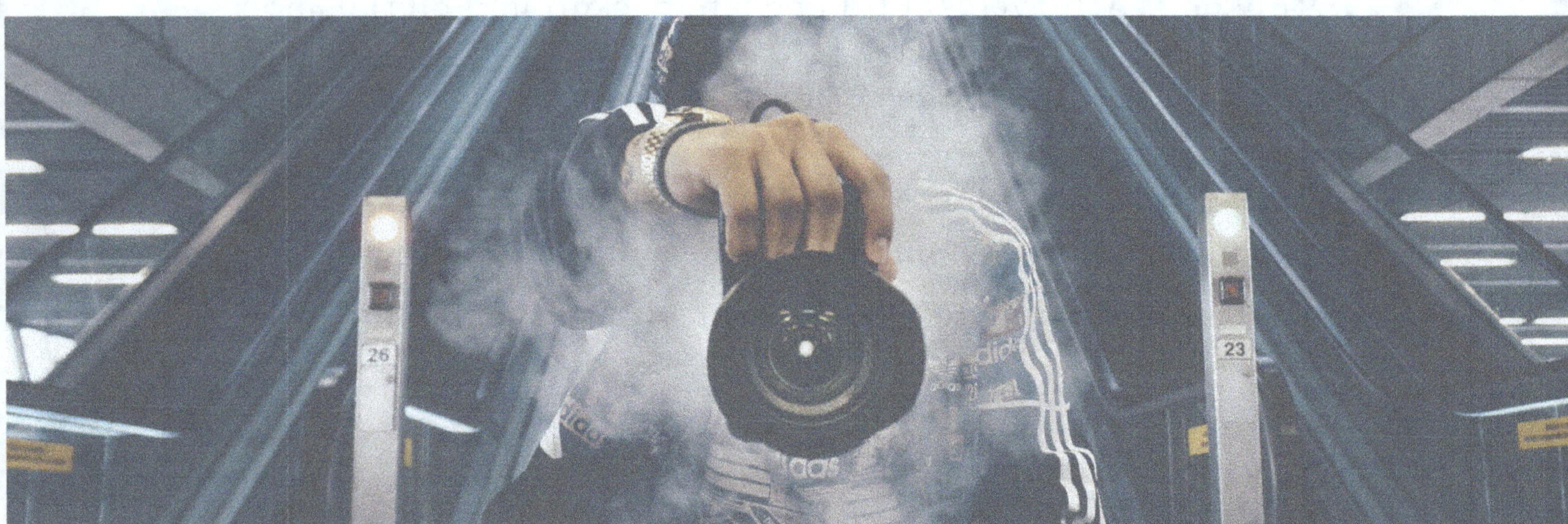

PERSONAL GROWTH & CREATIVE CHALLENGES

47. **365-Day Photo Challenge:** Commit to taking one photo every day for a year.
48. **Photography in Unusual Locations:** Challenge yourself to take captivating photos in unexpected places.
49. **No Editing Challenge:** Shoot with the intent of not editing the photos afterward.
50. **Limitation Challenge:** Choose one lens or camera setting and shoot exclusively with it for a day, week, or month.

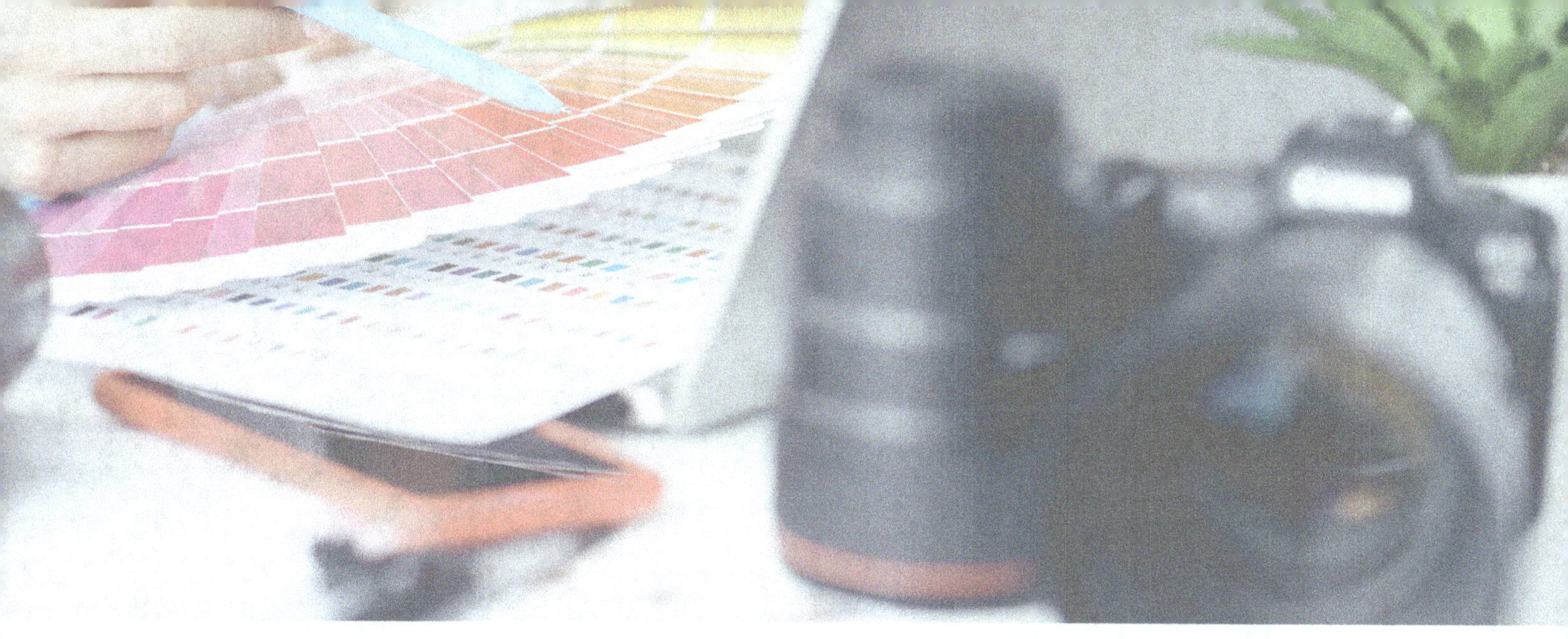

OTHER PHOTOGRAPHY PORTFOLIO BUILDING TIPS

- Collaborate with Models:

  - Work with models to build a strong portfolio of portrait photography, showcasing your ability to capture people's essence.

- Candid Moments:

  - Capture spontaneous, unposed moments to demonstrate your storytelling skills.

- .Before and After Photos:

  - Include image pairs that show your post-processing skills and the transformation of your photos.

TESTIMONIALS

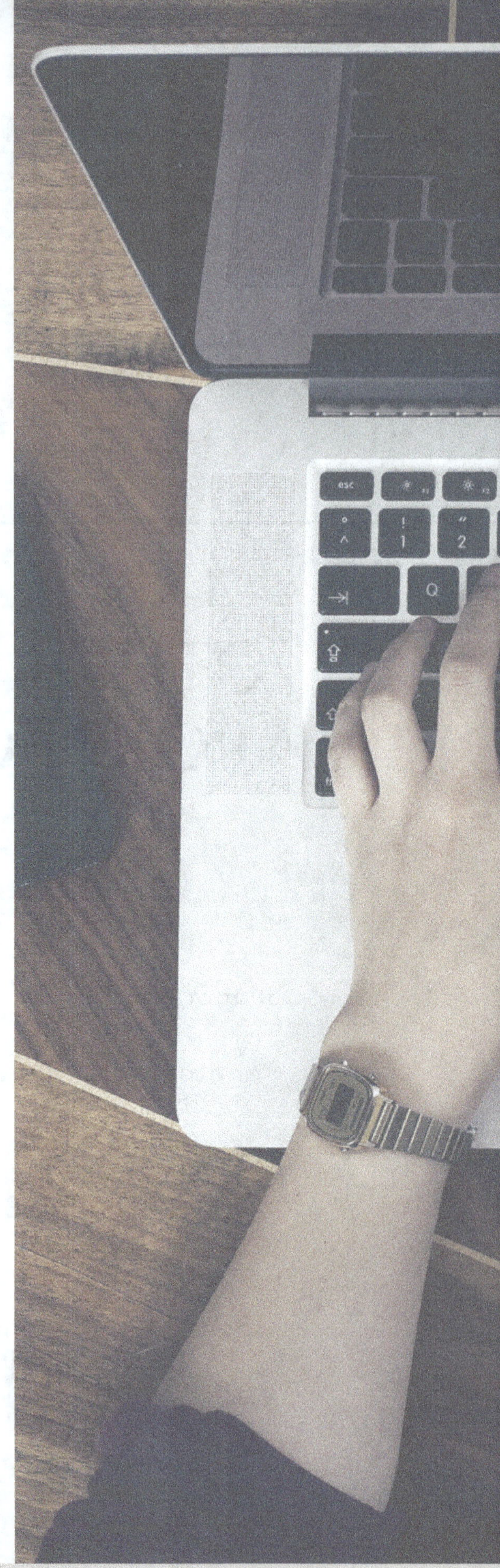

AS YOU BEGIN WORK WITH CLIENTS AND EXPAND YOUR PORTFOLIO, DON'T FORGET TO ASK CLIENTS FOR A TESTIMONIAL.

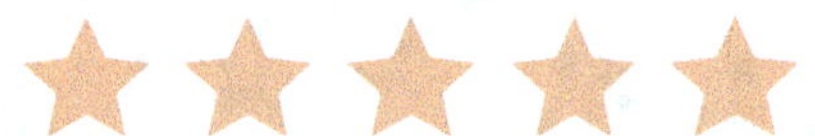

Send clients a link to a customer survey, your Facebook business page, or Google business listing and request a review.

Reviews help build small businesses by showcasing experience and building trust.

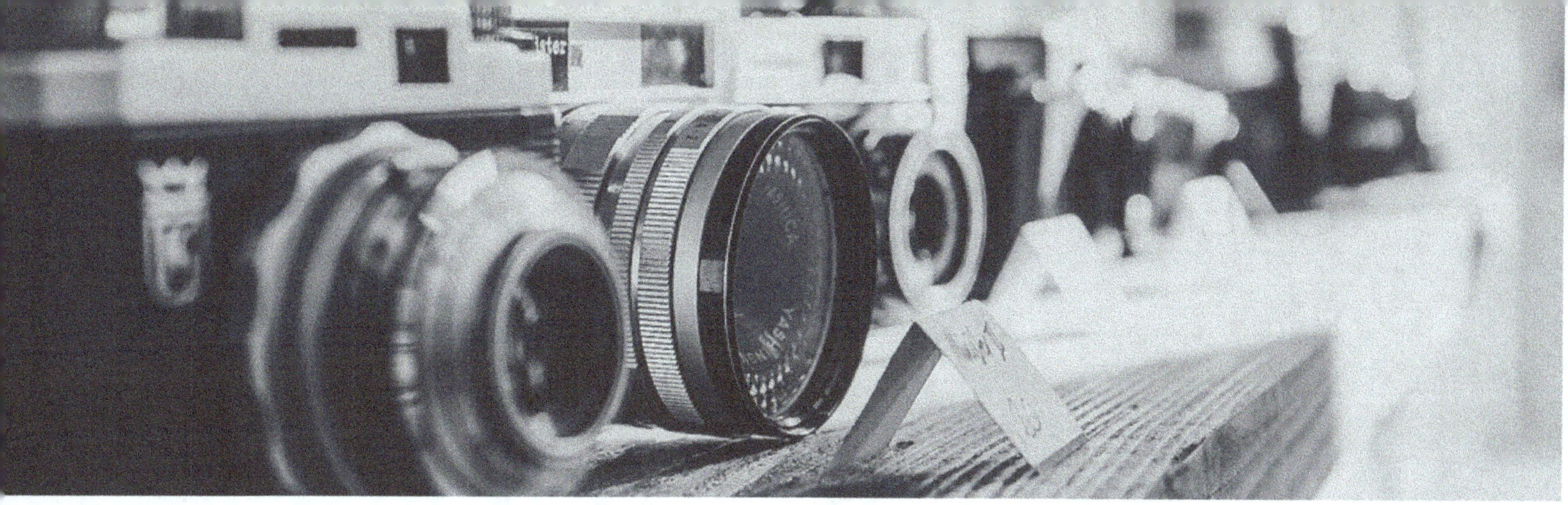

CONCLUSION

In the photography industry, a portfolio isn't just a collection of images; it's your visual identity, your journey, and your artistic testament. Remember that it's not just about displaying your skills; it's about telling a story, conveying emotions, and leaving a lasting impression.

Your portfolio is an ever-evolving canvas, a reflection of your growth as a photographer. It's a showcase of your unique perspective, your creativity, and your ability to capture moments that transcend time. So, continue to experiment, learn, and evolve as a photographer.

Crafting an outstanding portfolio is not a destination; it's a continuous journey. Embrace new challenges, seek inspiration in the world around you, and let your passion guide you. With each click of your shutter, you have the opportunity to add another masterpiece to your ever-expanding portfolio, one that will captivate viewers.

I hope these exercises have stretched your skills and expanded your imagination! Keep working, keep learning, and keep improving!

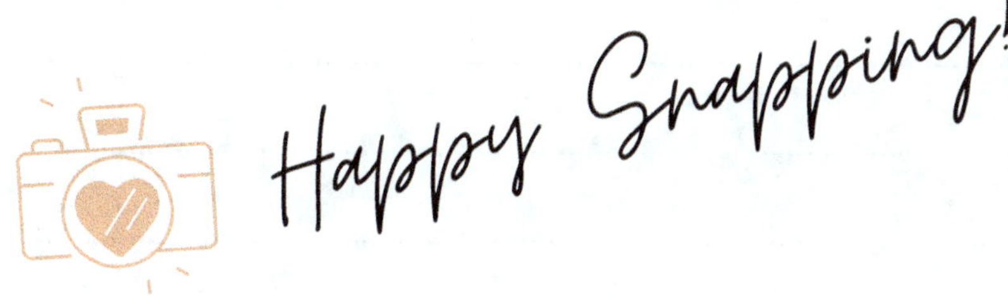

PORTFOLIO-BUILDING ACTIVITIES CHECKLIST

Month: .... Week: ....

Tasks	Su	Mo	Tu	We	Th	Fr	Sa
	✓						

YOUR NOTES:

YOUR NOTES:

THANK YOU FOR READING!

(DON'T FORGET TO LEAVE A REVIEW AFTER COMPLETING THE WORKBOOK)

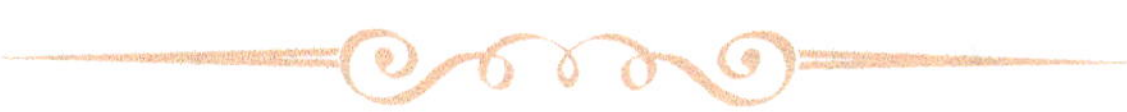

SHOP FOR MORE OF MY EBOOKS, WORKBOOKS, AND TOOLS ON AMAZON

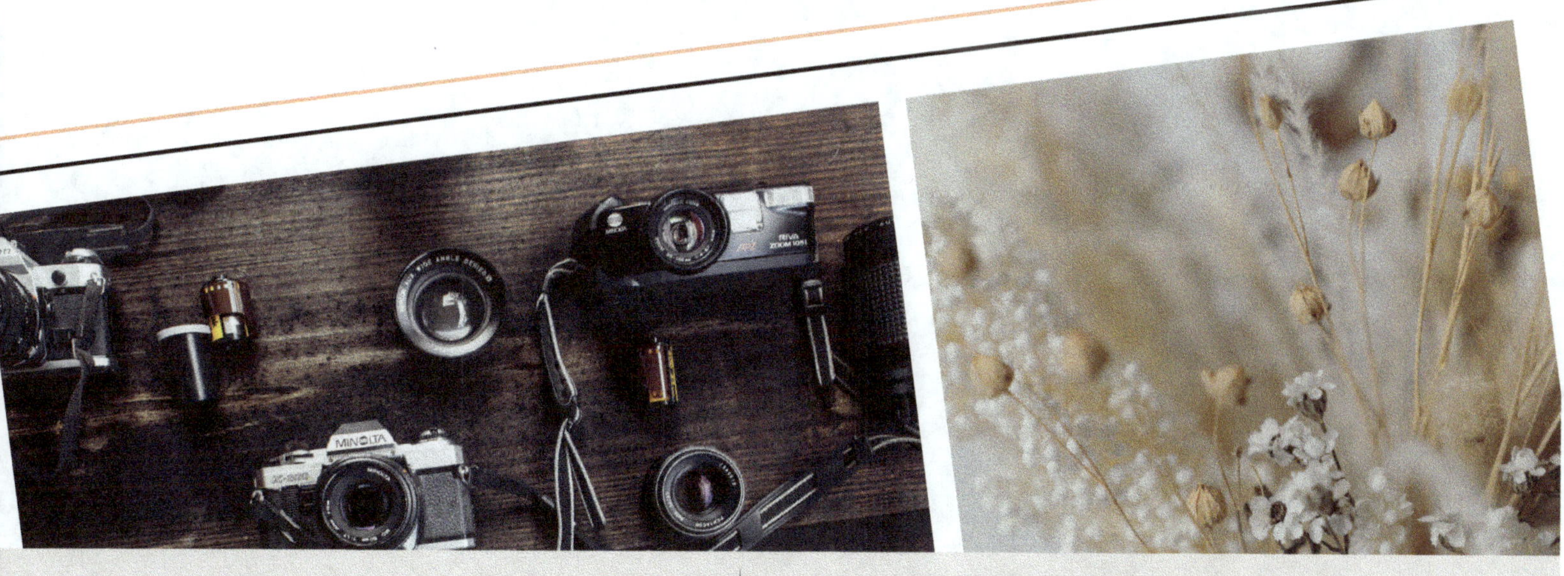

AMANDA OTIS   PORTFOLIO WORKBOOK

www.ingramcontent.com/pod-product-compliance
Lightning Source LLC
Chambersburg PA
CBHW080508030726
47592CB00011B/3297